Lizzie McGuire

Volume 7

CONTENTS

Lizzie McGuire

LIZZIE McGUIRE:
A typical 14-year-old girl who has her fair share of bad hair days and embarrassing moments. Luckily, Lizzie knows how to admit when she's wrong, back up her friends and stand up for herself.

Lizzie's alter-ego, who says and does all the thing Lizzie's afraid to.

MIRANDA:
Lizzie's best friend.

GORDO:
Lizzie and Miranda's smart, slightly weird friend who's always there to help in a crisis.

Lizzie McGuire

Volume 7

Series created by Terri Minsky

Over the Hill

written by Allison Taylor

Just Friends

written by Doug Tuber & Tim Maile

TOKYOPOP®

HAMBURG • LONDON • LOS ANGELES • TOKYO

Contributing Editors - Robert Buscemi & Amy Court Kaemon
Graphic Design & Lettering - Monalisa J. de Asis
Graphic Artists - Tomás Montalvo-Lagos and Jennifer Nunn-Iwai
Cover Layout - Patrick Hook

Editor - Erin Stein
Digital Imaging Manager - Chris Buford
Pre-Press Manager - Antonio DePietro
Production Managers - Jennifer Miller & Mutsumi Miyazaki
Art Director - Matt Alford
Managing Editor - Jill Freshney
VP of Production - Ron Klamert
President & C.O.O. - John Parker
Publisher & C.E.O. - Stuart Levy

Email: info@tokyopop.com
Come visit us online at www.TOKYOPOP.com

A TOKYOPOP® Cine-Manga™
TOKYOPOP Inc.
5900 Wilshire Blvd., Suite 2000, Los Angeles, CA 90036

Lizzie McGuire Volume 7

ISBN: 1-59182-573-3

First TOKYOPOP printing: August 2004

10 9 8 7 6 5 4 3 2 1

Printed in Canada

CHARACTER BIOS

KATE:
Miranda and Lizzie's now-popular ex-friend.

ETHAN:
The coolest kid in school. Lizzie has a crush on him.

MATT:
Lizzie's little brother, who spends most of his time driving her crazy.

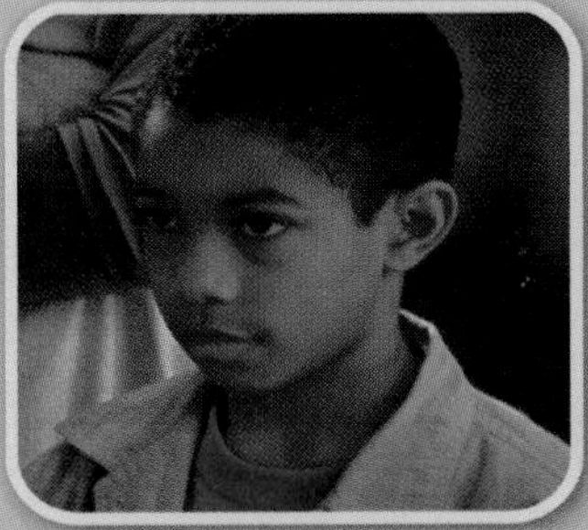

LANNY:
Matt's best friend.

LIZZIE'S MOM:
She only wants the best for Lizzie, but sometimes she tries a little too hard.

LIZZIE'S DAD:
He loves Lizzie, though he doesn't always know how to relate to her.

Lizzie McGuire

Over the Hill

Gordo makes films, Miranda makes music. In fact, everyone but Lizzie seems to have a special talent. And when Lizzie has a horrible nightmare about her future (or lack thereof), the hunt is on to find her life's true calling.

At Lizzie's school...
Miranda, what would you call this color?
Goldish greenish...
Pinkish...
How about just "gold"?
Gold? Just gold? It took me an hour to mix this color last night, Gordo. I think it deserves a name that says...
..."Throw your hands in the air, and wave 'em like you just don't care."
I was thinking more like L to the Izzie, Mc to the Guire.
The sad thing is, I understood that.

Hey! I could write a dictionary that translates English into "Girl-ish." I could make millions!
"Girl-ish"?
Okay, maybe that's not so P.C.
How do you women feel about the word "fem-bonics"?
Let's see what Ethan thinks.
ETHAN!
Hey, guys!
Lizzie, I'm feeling those gold nails.

"Gold"! It sounds so much better when he says it!
"Gold"! Oh, what a perfect name! I was wondering what to call it!
WHAT?
Little Lizzie. So economical. Did you give yourself that haircut, too?
I think it's sweet that you're supporting Cara like this!
Huh?
Didn't you hear? My pal Cara Gunther won a spot on the Olympic diving team.
Didn't get the memo.

Oh, I totally knew. I was going to ask Cara how many bottles of "Gold Medal Gunther" she needed me to mix.
Let's go, Ethan!
BYE!
Smooth.
Nice save.
Never let 'em see you sweat!

That night at home...
So now he's the ghost of the creepy old lumberjack?
Correction, Mom—he's not a ghost. He's the undead. Doomed to walk the Earth by day.
And by night, he feeds on people's brains as the Bonelicker. Look, he's wearing a bib.
He doesn't want to get any brain-stain on his shirt when he's chomping on skulls!
AAAH! AAAH!
Now, you let us know if this gets too scary for you, okay?
Puh-leez.
NO! PLEASE! AAAAAH!

...and then the dentist took this stick thing and scraped it over my tongue. You wouldn't believe all the gunk...
Uh, Lizzie, I gotta go. I've got gunk of my own to do.
Me too.
Since when did you guys get so busy?
I'm printing out flyers for my screening Saturday. You are coming, right?
And I'm practicing for my recital. It's Sunday, don't forget.
Oh yeah, I've got to practice for that big festival of absolutely nothing I'm doing this weekend.
Don't worry, you'll find something to do. You always do.
I gotta jet.
Ciao for now.
I'll find something to do.

No, no, don't go in there! Why do they keep going in there?
Shh!! This is the classic scene.
I'VE GOT A BONE TO CHEW WITH YOU!!
How's that for brain-stain, Matt? Matt?
Matt? Matt?
AAAAH! AAAAAAH!
AAAAH! AAAAH! NO! AAAH!
No! Mom, don't be silly. I wasn't sitting close enough, and look, we're missing the opening of the graves!!
That's it. Turn it off.

We'll follow the teen Internet mogul as she launches her newest Web site. The dough just keeps rolling in for this cute teen millionaire.
CLICK
CLICK
...champion was really upset by a 12-year-old genius newcomer...
...and it's on to MIT for the 11-year-old college graduate!
He'll have a Ph.D. before he gets zits!
He'll have a Ph.D. before I get zits!
Stick a fork in you, you're done.
CLICK

I think that was just way too scary for him.
Oh, he's fine.
I used to watch scary movies when I was his age.
I turned out okay.
OH, YEAH?

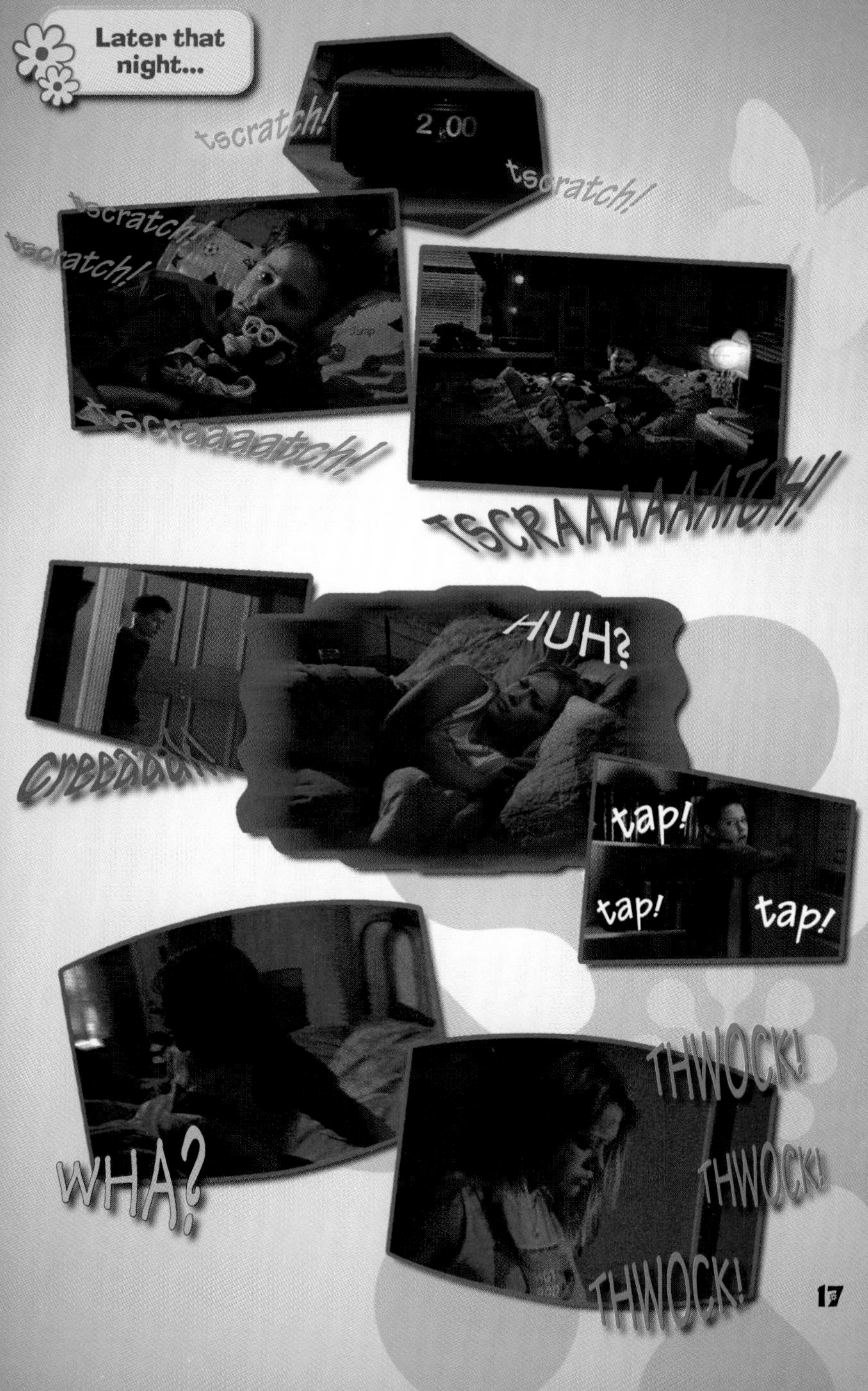
Later that night...
2:00
tscratch!
tscratch!
tscratch!
tscratch!
tscraaaaatch!
HUH?
tap!
tap!
tap!
WHA?
THWOCK!
THWOCK!
THWOCK!

PHEW!
Matt? What are you doing?
There's a presence in this house!
Ghost-pimple!
What's wrong, honey? Can't sleep?
Sixth Sense here is seeing dead people again. I'll let you guys handle this one.

Come on, son. Back to bed.
Good night.
I'll leave this to you.
No! But that room is alive with the howling of the undead!
Come on, son.
No! No! No!

A few hours later...
AUGUST 2004
AUGUST 2036
Thank you for landing on Burger Planet!
I should have invested in municipal... high yield...small cap...
...I should have gotten a piggy bank.
Welcome to Burger Planet! May I take your order?
Five orders of curly fries, please.
Thank you. Drive around to the window.

...world famous concert violinist Miranda Sanchez performs for the Lincoln Center audience.
CLAP!
CLAP!
CLAP!
HUH?
Five orders of curly fries, sir?
Better make it six. Gordo loves his fries.
Gordo? As in David Gordon, the famous director? He's in that car?
Gordo? Curly fries?

You didn't hear it from me.
I've got to see him!! I've gotta see Gordo!
OOF!
Back off, grandma! He's a very important person.
I know, but you don't understand. Gordo and I went to middle school together. We used to be best buds!
ARGH!
TAP!
TAP!
Gordo! It's me!! Lizzie!!!
TAP!
What was *that* all about?
Some nut job. Couldn't figure out what she wanted to do in life until it was way too late.
Did she say her name was Lizzie? Didn't I used to know a Lizzie? No, I guess not.

Gordo! Gordo! Remember me? Lizzie! Lizzie McGuire!
THWAP!
THWAP!
Gordo!!! Don't leave me!!
SCREEEEEECH!
AAGH!!
AAAGH!
AAGH!
It's just a dream, Lizzie. Get it out of your mind.

And when that doesn't work... Mommy!
Mom, Dad! We need to talk! Now.
Creeeaaaak!
CLICK
Isn't it time you stopped running to Mom and Dad for every little thing?

I guess you're right.
Oh, by the way—"Hello, Clarice."
Don't do that!!
What's wrong, sweetie?
What's wrong? Gordo is in a limo, and I'm a lonely old loser truck stop waitress for the rest of my life! What are you going to do about it??!!
We'll leave this to you.

Why do moms think that hot chocolate fixes everything?
GLUG!
GLUG!
Because it does.
Okay, now. What's on your mind, sweetie?
Apparently, nothing. And you two haven't done anything to help.
What did we do?

It's what you didn't do, Dad.
While I've been singing "Oops, I Did It Again" into a hairbrush, people are going to the Olympics and playing for the governor and—and Spielberg-ing!
Spielberg-ing? Did Gordo do another movie? He is so talented.
Not helping!
Is this about that Gunther girl, the diver?
This is about the day in kindergarten where we all decided what we were going to be. Where was I?
And where were you two?
Do you remember that rhythmic gymnastics thing you did last year? You rocked.
We were behind you a thousand percent. But you told us you weren't passionate about it.

And thanks for picking right now to start saying "rocked," Dad.
But if you made me stick to it, I might be going to the Olympics too.
That's why I'm nothing, Mom!
But honey, we can't force you into "being" something.
Continue...
You're fantastic, you're smart, you're talented, you're...
...a little insecure right now.
Go back to "talented," then stop.

Listen, when you find out what it is that you want to be, you won't need us to tell you.
And you certainly don't need to figure it out tonight.
AHEM!
Unless, of course, you'd like to. We're here for you!
Mom, Dad, face it. There are already 50 million things I can never be!
SLUURP!
AAAAAH!!
I burnt my tongue! Now I can never be a food critic!

The next day...
Thanks for coming. Matt won't go near his room. He says he senses something in the house.
BRRRR!
This is out of control.
Just let them work it out their way.
Oh, yeah, that's easy for you to say. You get to go play softball while I'm stuck here.
Hey, I didn't make up the schedule. It just worked out. Bye.

...and then the car zooms off—leaving me behind to talk into a clown's mouth for the rest of my life.
HUH?
My road dogs! They've always got my back.
Did you say that I have a limo driver who gets me curly fries?
My hair is long and gray like my *abuela*?
Maybe it's time for a new set of road dogs.
Can we focus here, you guys? My life needs a plan. You guys don't know what it's like seeing everyone pass you by.
Nobody's passing you by. You're just good at a lot of different things.

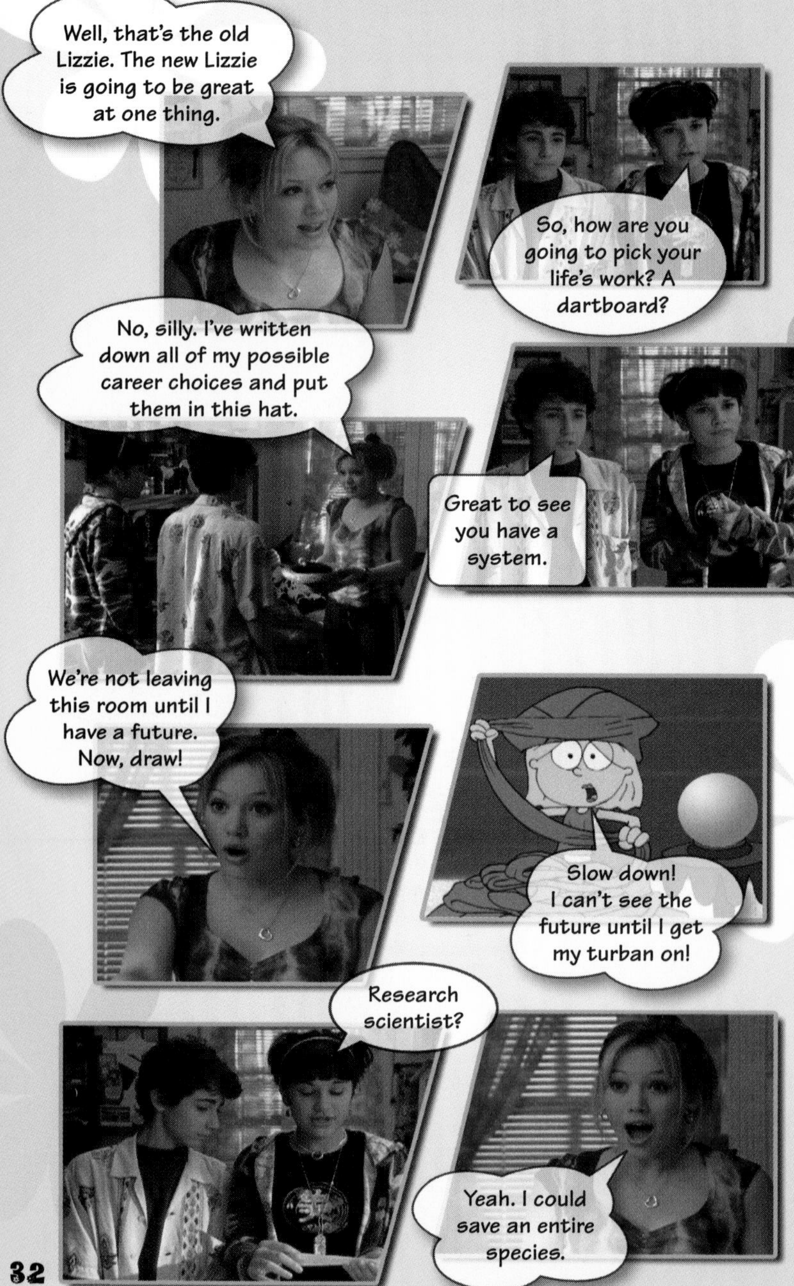

Well, that's the old Lizzie. The new Lizzie is going to be great at one thing.
So, how are you going to pick your life's work? A dartboard?
No, silly. I've written down all of my possible career choices and put them in this hat.
Great to see you have a system.
We're not leaving this room until I have a future. Now, draw!
Slow down! I can't see the future until I get my turban on!
Research scientist?
Yeah. I could save an entire species.

I would like to announce that after years of work, we have recovered and cloned DNA from the last wild bald eagle.
Thanks to our research, our national symbol will once again fly free, and...
Lovely. God bless America. Now, can we wrap this up?
I've got a wax at three, and it is now...
WOOSH!
Noooooooo!!
Noooooooo!!

AAAAH!
WOOSH!
Yes!
FAP!
OH,
WOO-HOO!
That year, I could win the Nobel Prize and the Golden Glove.
Works for me. Now, about the near future... did I hear some talk of curly fries?

I'm not finished. Draw.
A NASCAR driver?
I like the little jumpsuit with all the patches.
GO, LIZZIE, GO!!
I have a need for speed.
Whatever happened to being something normal like a doctor or a lawyer?
Well, blood makes me kinda squirmy, and law is so...
YAWN!!

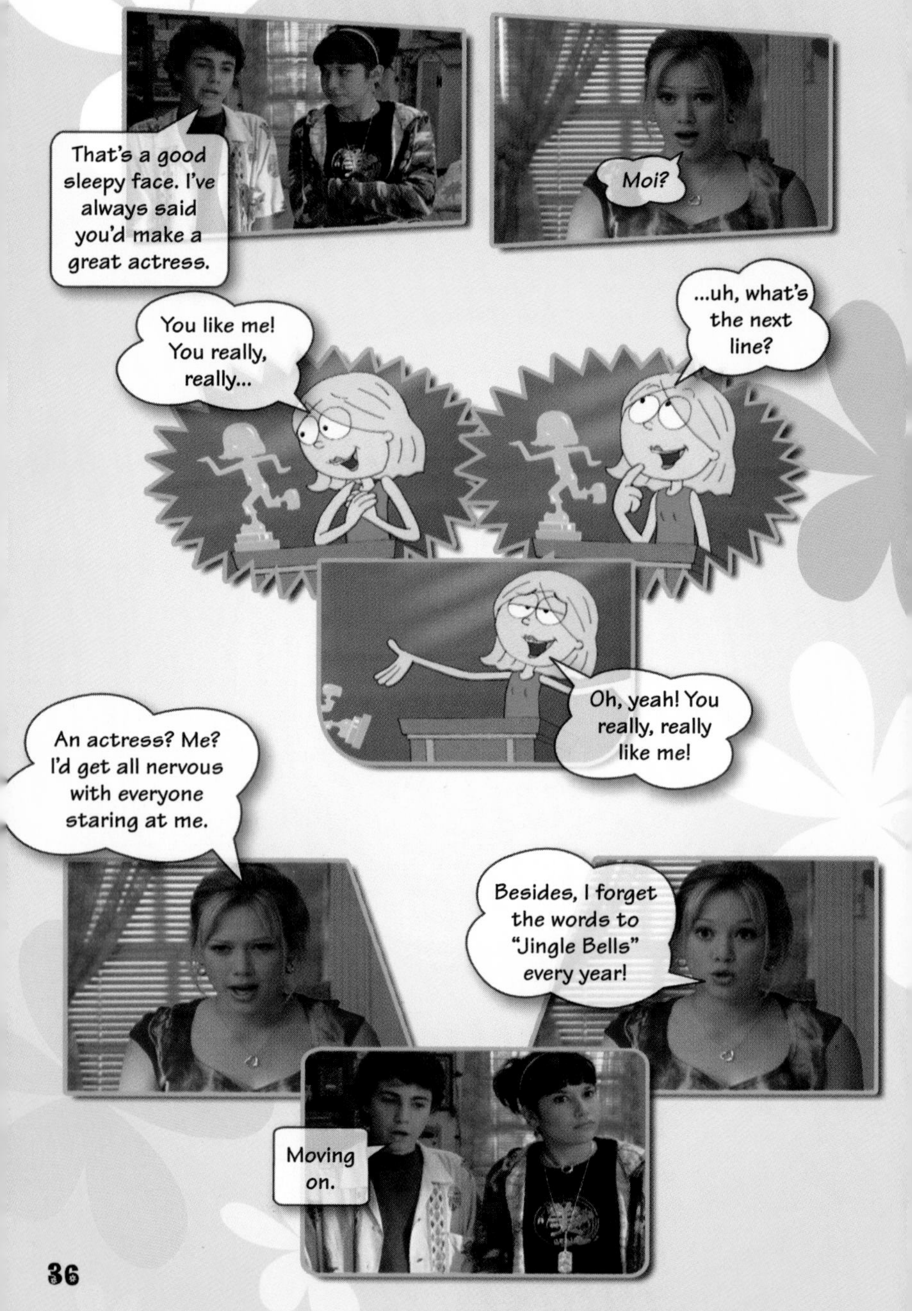
That's a good sleepy face. I've always said you'd make a great actress.
Moi?
You like me! You really, really...
...uh, what's the next line?
Oh, yeah! You really, really like me!
An actress? Me? I'd get all nervous with everyone staring at me.
Besides, I forget the words to "Jingle Bells" every year!
Moving on.

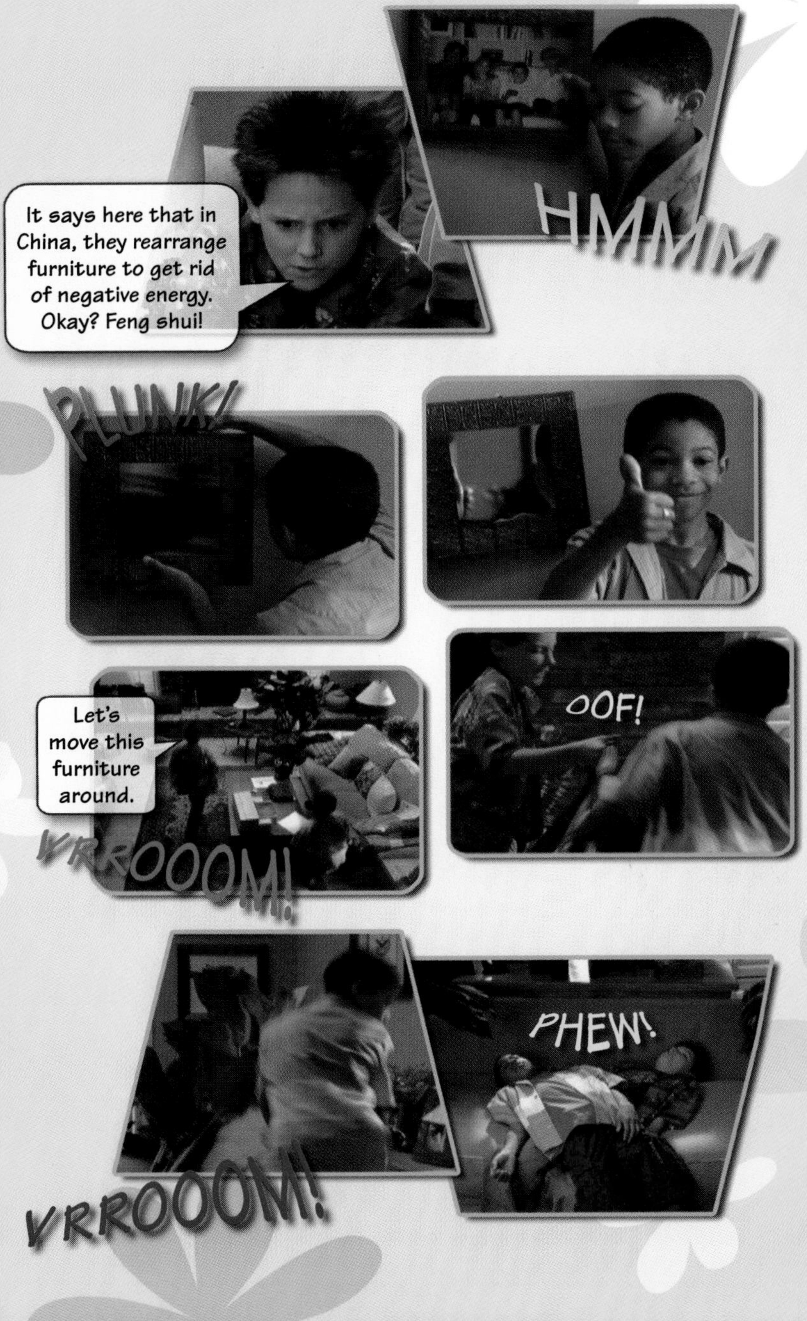

It says here that in China, they rearrange furniture to get rid of negative energy. Okay? Feng shui!
HMMMM
PLUNK!
Let's move this furniture around.
VRROOOM!
OOF!
VRROOOM!
PHEW!

Hours later...
Look, Mom, the spirit flies in the window, crashes into the lamp shade, bounces off the mirror and lands in the cactus. That ghost is toast.
GASP!
If you don't put all this stuff back before your father gets home, you are also going be toast.
Oh, and speaking of toast, we made these garlic necklaces to ward off vampires.
I know. We're being overcautious, but there's no arguing with Lanny.
WHAP!
I wouldn't dare.

Hello. Hey, honey. No, um, the game just finished. Yeah, I can bring some garlic home.
You're wearing garlic? No, I know I told him to figure it out. Okay, okay. *I'll* figure it out.
Honey?
CLICK!
Hey, guys...
...you wanna make a quick 20 bucks?

Okay. Last one.
Stay-at-home mom?
Somebody's gotta do it, right?
I'd get up and get the kids breakfast.
Freak.
Dork.
Kids, cut it out!
And at the end of the day, my gorgeous husband would come home from work...

AGGH!
Why are you yelling?
Because I am sick of your girl talk! Enough about your future husband, okay?!
Yeah, well, you don't exactly see me doing cartwheels, either!
What?

Emergency subject change!
I don't know what I'm saying. Just draw!
The hat's empty. So what's it gonna be?
This is so silly, isn't it? I can't pick my future out of a hat.
I'm glad I didn't have to tell you.
So, how do I do it?
You've got your movies, and you've got your music—you guys are set for the rest of your lives.
The rest of our lives? Lizzie, I may never be a professional musician.
Exactly. She might never be a professional musician!

No, you are supposed to say you might never be a professional director.
Are we here to talk crazy or are we here to help Lizzie?
You know, it just makes me nervous seeing you guys change while I stay the same all the time.
Not according to my shoe size.
Stay the same? Lizzie, you're not the same as last year!
Did you see the way you just marched up to Ethan yesterday?

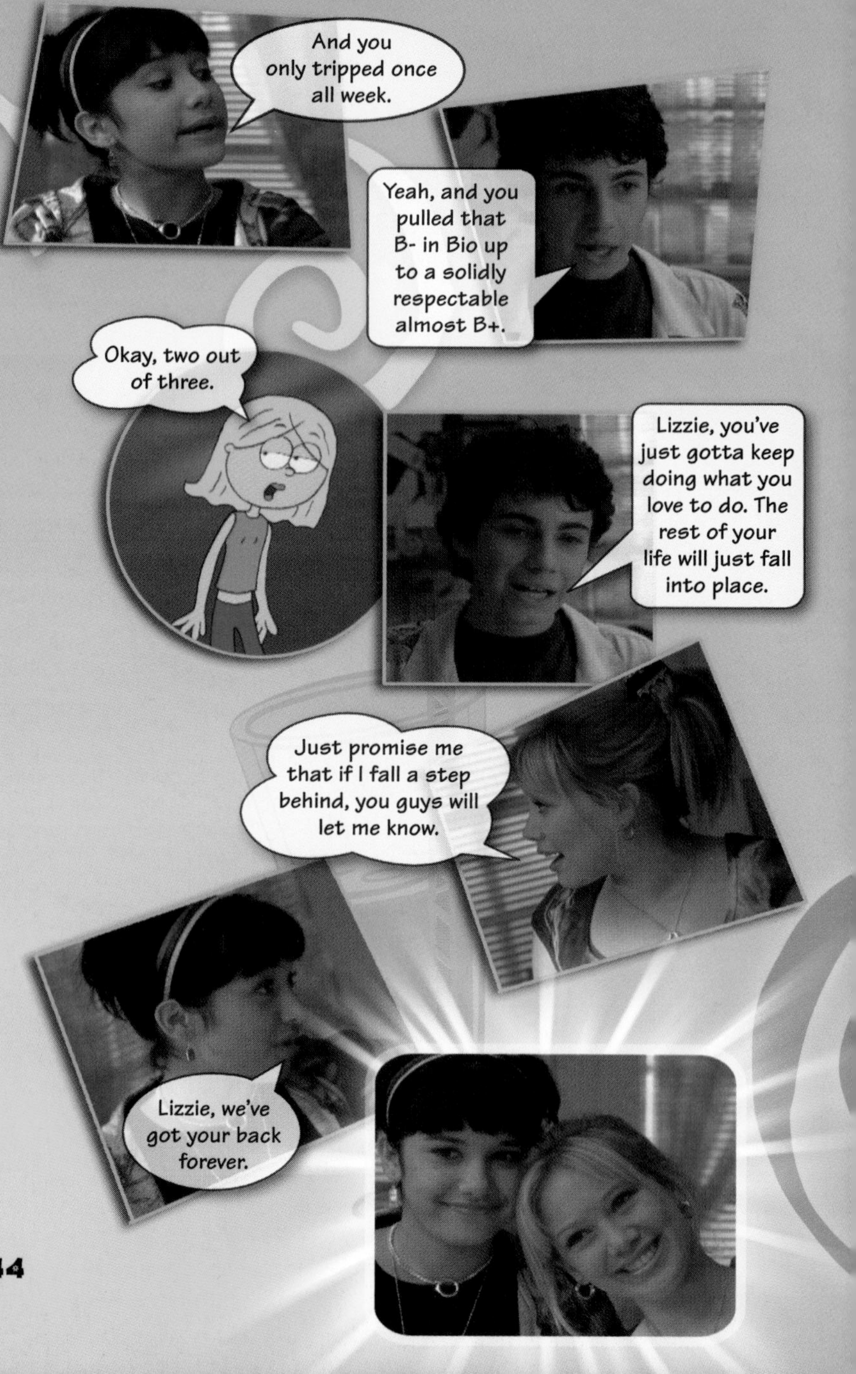
And you only tripped once all week.
Yeah, and you pulled that B- in Bio up to a solidly respectable almost B+.
Okay, two out of three.
Lizzie, you've just gotta keep doing what you love to do. The rest of your life will just fall into place.
Just promise me that if I fall a step behind, you guys will let me know.
Lizzie, we've got your back forever.

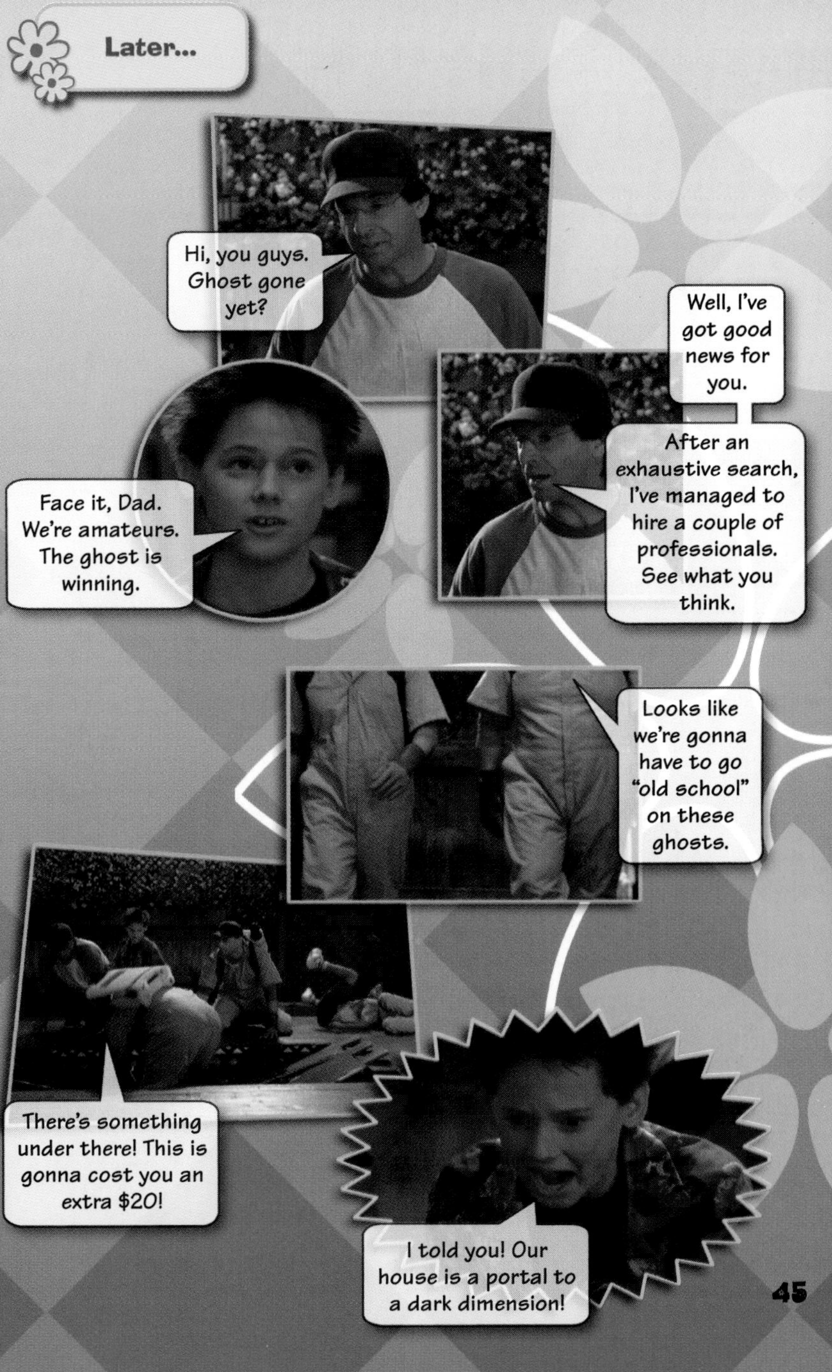
Later...
Hi, you guys. Ghost gone yet?
Face it, Dad. We're amateurs. The ghost is winning.
Well, I've got good news for you.
After an exhaustive search, I've managed to hire a couple of professionals. See what you think.
Looks like we're gonna have to go "old school" on these ghosts.
There's something under there! This is gonna cost you an extra $20!
I told you! Our house is a portal to a dark dimension!

What is happening out here?
Not too close, honey. Careful.
MOM!
Look into the face of evil.
YRAP!
YRUFF!
YRAP!
Puppies!! Puppies!!!

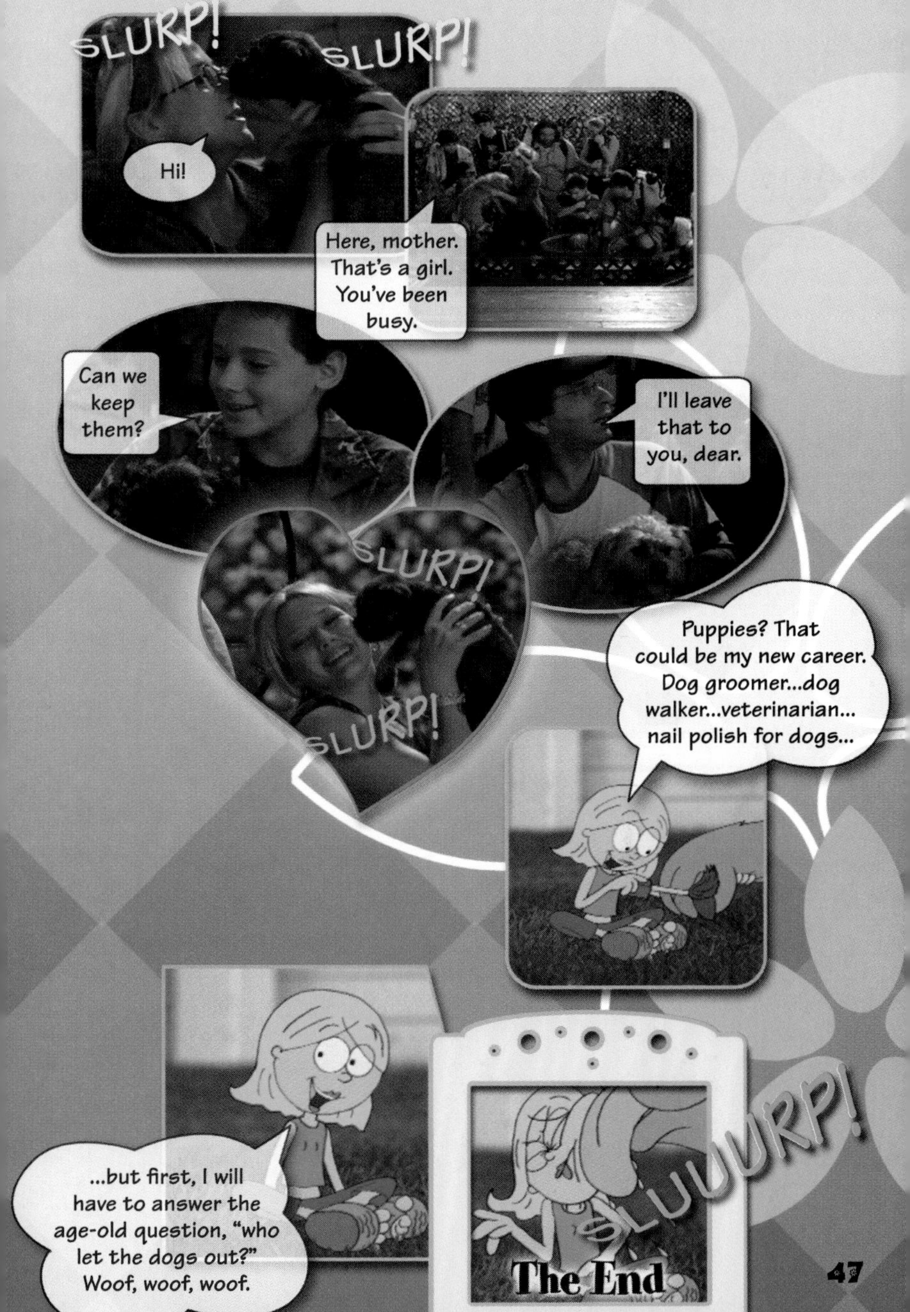
SLURP!
SLURP!
Hi!
Here, mother. That's a girl. You've been busy.
Can we keep them?
I'll leave that to you, dear.
SLURP!
SLURP!
Puppies? That could be my new career. Dog groomer...dog walker...veterinarian... nail polish for dogs...
...but first, I will have to answer the age-old question, "who let the dogs out?" Woof, woof, woof.
SLUUURP!
The End

Lizzie
McGuire

Just Friends

With the Girls Ask Guys dance just around the corner, Lizzie's on a mission to give herself a total makeover. If she can change into exactly what Ethan's looking for in a girlfriend, he won't be able to resist her, right?

At Lizzie's school...
Did you hear? Larry Tudgeman has finally cracked.
I heard him talking about going to the dance on Friday with Kate.
It's his diet. He lives on fish sticks and cream soda.
He hasn't cracked. He's just excited about the Girls Ask Guys dance. This is his big chance.
Okay, but does he actually think that Kate is gonna ask him?
Okay, he's cracked.
You know, Lizzie, no one's asked Ethan to the dance yet.
Yes!
You should ask him.

Why not? You're always talking about how much you like the guy, but you never, ever do anything about it.
No!
Lizzie, Ethan obviously likes you. So just ask him. He'll say yes.
You know what, you're right. I don't have to wait for him to ask. I mean, I have my own power!
I can see it, and I can be it!
WHOOPS!
KA-THUNK!
HEE HEE!
Okay, I didn't see that.

At lunch...
So, I've been practicing my speech to ask Ethan out. You be Ethan, okay?
Yo, Liz-zie.
So, Ethan, the dance is coming up soon...
My cousin had a hamster named Joey!
...and I was wondering if anyone had asked you yet?
Yesterday, I learned how to tie my shoes. But now I forgot!
Okay, Gordo, stop, this is serious.

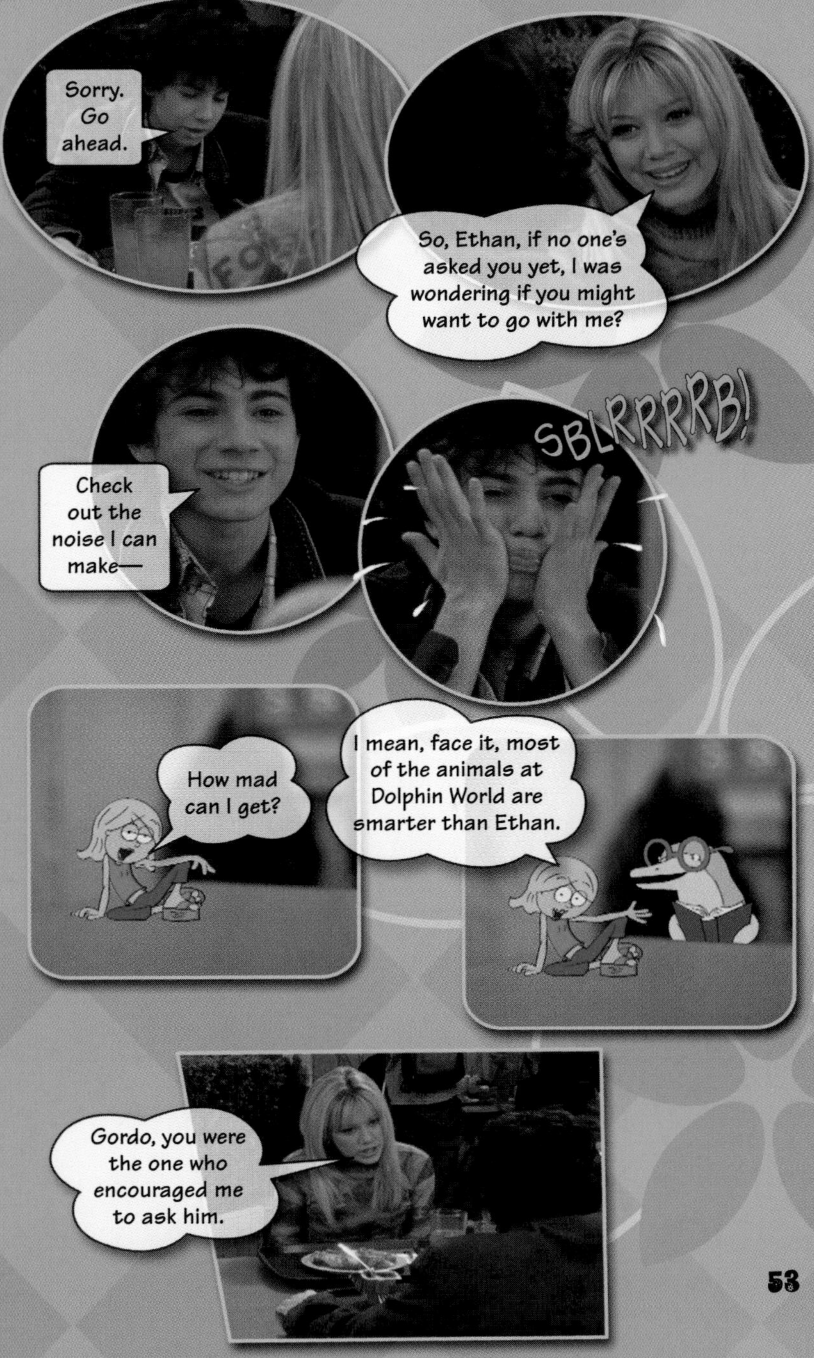
Sorry. Go ahead.
So, Ethan, if no one's asked you yet, I was wondering if you might want to go with me?
Check out the noise I can make—
SBLRRRRB!
How mad can I get?
I mean, face it, most of the animals at Dolphin World are smarter than Ethan.
Gordo, you were the one who encouraged me to ask him.

Do you have a date for the dance yet?
Eh, I'm not too worried about it. I'm at a stage in my life where girls just don't value what I have to offer.
But I'll have women all over me after I've invented my new software application, bought a jet, and am running five corporations from my private island.
You know, when I'm, like, 20. 'Til then, I just have to lay low and get plenty of rest.
SCHOOL
Oh my gosh, here he comes!
TONIGHT!
Hey, Ethan. How's it going?

Lizzie, Lizzie, Lizzie, my day is proceeding with fineness.
So, the dance is coming up and I was wondering if anyone had asked you yet.
Please say no, please say no, please say no!
No. So far, I'm paddling my kayak alone.
Oh!
This is it. I'm about to dive into the waters of romance.

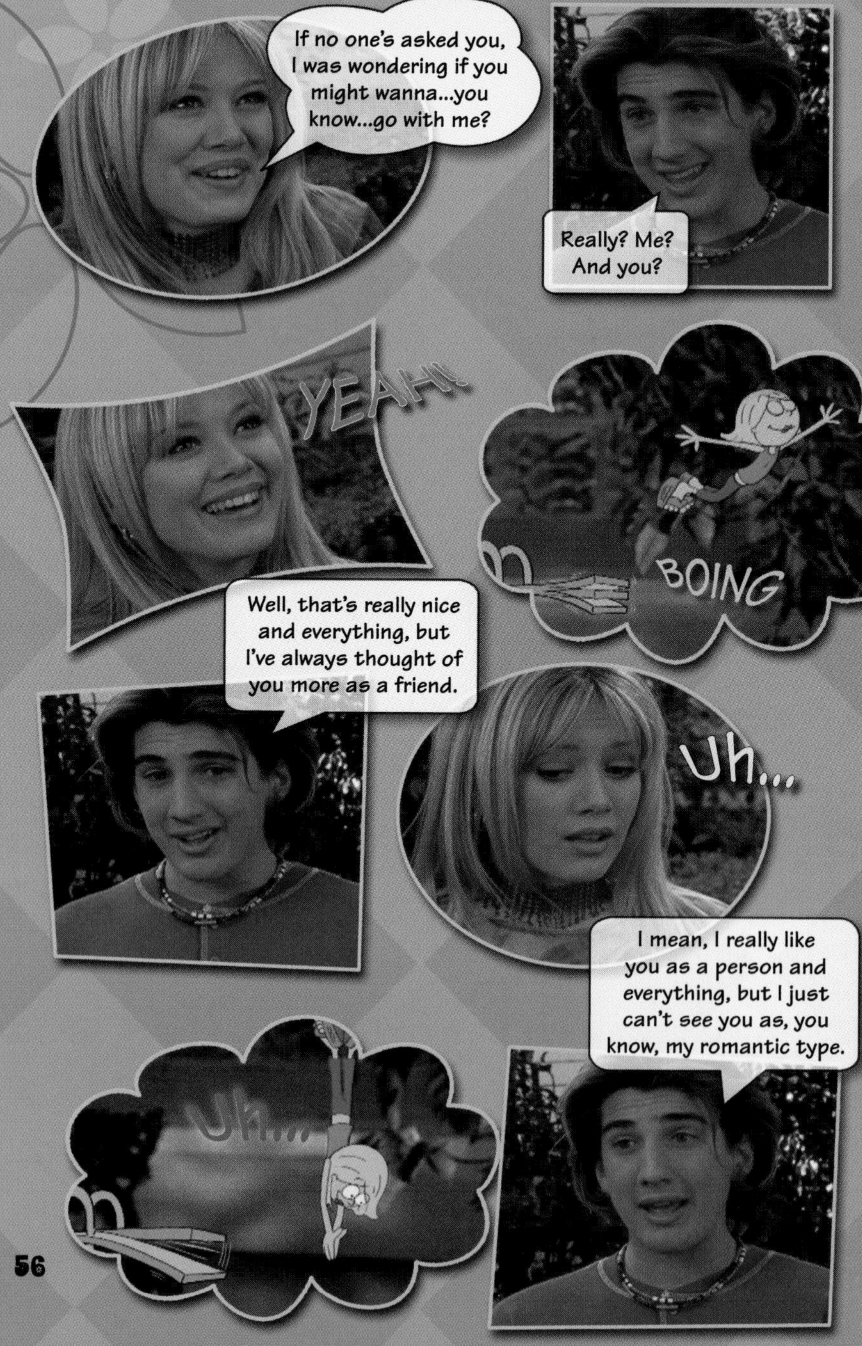
If no one's asked you, I was wondering if you might wanna...you know...go with me?
Really? Me? And you?
YEAH!!
BOING
Well, that's really nice and everything, but I've always thought of you more as a friend.
Uh...
I mean, I really like you as a person and everything, but I just can't see you as, you know, my romantic type.
Uh...

WHUNK!
OOOOH!
That's cool, then. I see you as a friend too. So, we'll be friends.
WHAT?
Coolness. So, I'll see you later.
HMPH!!

That afternoon at home...
Evil Dr. Matt's Sinister Transformation Formula nears completion.
Lanny! Bring me... the vanilla extract!
HEE HEE HEE!
Matt, what are you doing?
Inventing a potion that will usher in thousands of years of evil.
Okay, well, don't break anything.
Now, Lanny—throw the switch!
HA HA HA HA!
WHIRZ! WHIRZZZ!

Enough!
GLUG!
GLUG!
SLUUUUURP!
COUGH!
COUGH!
COUGH!
Actually, you know, that's very good.
Don't say another word, Lanny. Cause, as usual, you're completely correct.
Forget a thousand years of evil—we can sell this to our friends and make a fortune.

Where does Ethan get off, turning you down?
I don't know. I mean, I just always thought he kind of liked me.
Well, he does like you. He just doesn't "like you" like you.
But why not? I mean, I'm decent-looking.
You're very pretty.
And I'm a nice person.
You're a great person.
And I'm wild and unpredictable.

Uhhh...
You're a great person.
No, I bet Ethan's looking for some wild, crazy, Drew Barrymore-type of girl.
No. Last year he liked Denice Palmer, and she's even duller than you.
HUH?
Not to say that you're dull, of course. You're just...not Ethan's type.
But why can't I be? I mean, I can change. I can be anything that he's looking for.
That's right. He wants a party girl, I can be a party girl.

He wants artsy, I can be artsy.
He wants intellectual...
Who am I kidding? Ethan can't even spell "intellectual."
But what *is* he looking for? What do you even know about the guy?
Well, I know he's a total hottie.
Well, *there's* a rock-solid foundation. We'll go from there.

The next day...
There you go, chief.
Lanny, I think we're on our way to being the hosts of the hottest spot in town.
ZOWIE!
Welcome!
CLINK!
Keep mixing, Lanny.

Okay! Do you see Ethan?
Uh...got him.
Well, who's he talking to? What's he doing? What can we tell about him that we don't already know?
Well...He's giving some of his sandwich to a pigeon.
He likes nature! I can talk to him about that.
Okay. Some more pigeons are coming over to get in on it. There are lots and lots of pigeons...
They're kind of swarming him. He's trying to get away. He's running. They're chasing him!
Run, Ethan, run! Aw, he just ran into a pole.
So...he likes nature and he's nearsighted. Okay, time for some closer surveillance.

Back at school...
Hey, Ethan, what's up?
Hey, Gordon.
So...girls. They're great, right?
Aw, yeah! Girls are awesome.
Yeah, I'll say. So, you know what kind of girls I like? I like real sophisticated types.
Like Britney Spears!
Yeah. Sure. So, what kind of girls do you like?
I always liked mysterious women. It's like they know something you don't, but you really want to know what that is.
So, you like girls who know things that you don't. You know, that doesn't really narrow it down very much.

You know, like the type of girls in old detective movies. They're all quiet and dangerous, but you just can't stay away.
Right. I got you.
You know, I never really get to talk about this kind of stuff.
It's kind of nice having someone to talk about it with. Maybe we should hang out more often.
Naw, I don't think so. See ya.
Mysterious, quiet type...
...we need more.

FAP!
FAP!

HMMMM!

CLICK

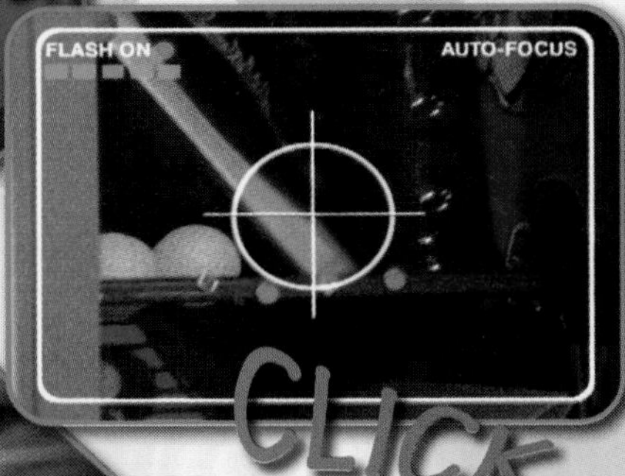
FLASH ON
AUTO-FOCUS
CLICK

SWIPE!

Take this!
HAND-OFF!
19TH GREEN
THE RIGHT CLUB
HMMM
GLUG!
GLUG!
GOTCHA!

He loves Roald Dahl books. Especially *Charlie and the Chocolate Factory*. He loves the Oompa-Loompas.
And we can't forget Ja Rule, grape soda and golf.
All right, I'm ready. Next time Ethan sees me, I'm gonna be the girl of his dreams.
A drop of grape soda...a teaspoon of golf...a pinch of Oompa-Loompa... and presto!
BLAMMO!
Okay, the formula needs some work.
Maybe a dash more Oompa-Loompa...

After school...
Club Flamingo
C'mon, this way.
Hey everyone!
Best table in the house for our big spenders.
Thanks, but we're here to see your sister.
Okay, well, thanks for coming by. Come again soon.
Deadbeats.

So, Ethan said he wanted mystery. Does this hat say "mystery woman" to you?
Are "mystery woman" and "bag lady" the same thing?
Then, no.
On the plus side, I snagged some golf magazines from my dad's waiting room. Knock yourself out.
Honey, are you gonna take up golf?
Um, yeah, Mom.
UH...
Does this have to do with making Ethan Craft like you?

You told her? Why would you tell her? All parents ever want to do is poke holes in things.
You know, poke, poke, poke, poke, poke!
WELL...
Here we go. All Mom wants to do is interfere in my life.
BLAH!
BLAH!
BLAH!
Mom, I really *like* golf. It's so... fast-paced.
You know, when I was your age, there was a group of kids that I really wanted to be friends with...

I changed the way I dressed, the way I talked, my whole personality…
…and I changed everything about myself to make them like me.
BLAH!
BLAH!
BLAH!
Hey, I guess she doesn't want to interfere. She just wants to tell some pointless story.
...but in the end, they still wouldn't hang out with me.
Wow. Really?
Maybe you didn't do it right. We're gonna be upstairs.
OH BOY!

The next day...
Why, hello, handsome.
Whoa. Lizzie, you look... whoa. Where'd you get those clothes?
Be mysterious, be mysterious...
Where do any of us get our clothes, Ethan?
That was mysterious. I have no idea what it meant.
I get mine at Dad 'N' Lad Outfitters over on Beacon Street.
Oh, do you?
Lizzie, golf this Saturday, right?
Yeah, see you at the first tee.

You like golf? I *love* golf! The problem is, I keep hooking my tee shots.
Oh, you know what really helps me? I listen to Ja Rule when I practice.
Oh, I love listening to that guy.
Here's the soda you wanted, Lizzie.
Thank you.
This is scary. Grape soda is, like, my favorite drink in the history of the world.
Oh, is it? Enjoy. Compliments of Lizzie McGuire.
WOW!

Drink up, Sunshine. It'll make a man out of you.
Uh-oh, Lanny. Look, it's Sonny Mazerowski. He's getting on everybody's case because no one goes over to his house anymore.
Sonny's parents have a 70-inch TV and a satellite dish. He charges people to watch in the afternoons.
Yeah, so?
You're costing me money. All of my customers are hanging out here.
So, I'm shutting you down. And I want your drink recipe.
Oh, yeah? Well, I want a solid gold Indy car. Doesn't mean it's gonna happen.

You can shut down, or you can start spending every lunch period at school in the trash can outside the cafeteria.
GULP!
Okay, everybody out! Everybody out! Out! Get out of here! Shoo!
Okay, what's in this?
Well, some strawber-ries...
And, uh, three cloves of garlic...half a cup of pickle juice...a jalapeño pepper...two cups of fish oil...

The next day at lunch...

I just can't believe that you like chili-pastrami-tortilla-dogs, too.
Oh, yeah, they're my favorite. Yum, yum, yum.
'Cause who really needs unclogged arteries anyway?
You know what would go perfect with this? An Everlasting Gobstopper.
Hey, that's from *Willy Wonka*. That's my favorite book. You know, it's incredible. We both like the same things.
It *is* incredible.
So, are you going to the dance with anyone tonight?

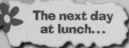

Nope. Still flying solo.
Um...we should go together.
Oh, uh...I thought we already understood each other about that. About how we're just gonna be friends.
Oh, well, uh... we just have so much in common.
I know. It's weird. It's like, if I wrote down everything we both like on paper, we'd be perfect for each other.
And I like you and all, but there's just no...
...oh, shoot—what's that subject in high school I'm never gonna pass?

Chemistry?
Yeah, there's just no chemistry. Does that make sense?
No. But I guess this stuff doesn't always make sense.
And the great thing about that is, I'm 14, so I only have to deal with this stuff for another 80 years.
I'm sorry.
Yeah. Me too.

That evening...
Maybe there's something better on another channel.
What? Oh. Sorry.
You okay, sweetie?
Uh... yeah...
Giving up golf, huh?
There's the silver lining. Golf pants look terrible on me.
Well, I like the old, non-golfing Lizzie better.

Yeah? Why didn't you say so? Why didn't you tell me changing to please Ethan was never gonna work?
Wait—my diary says you did. Never mind.
We're sorry the whole thing didn't work out for you.
If there's anything at all that we can do, you just let us know.
SIGH!
Huh. They don't want to control my life. They just want me to be happy.
Thanks.

SIGH!
There's really nothing more we can say to her. She'll bounce back from this.
You're probably right.
And since when did you become such an expert on teenage girls?
Well, I got dumped by enough of them. I got cut loose by every girl I ever liked.
Until I met the perfect woman.

So, uh, you got anymore of that Supersonic Tonic left?
Sure.
Ethan trouble?
Mmm-hmm.
You know, if you're going to drink this every time a guy dumps you, I'd better make a million gallons.

SIGH!
This is the part where you call me a squeaky runt or a spiky-haired weasel or something.
Sorry.
He didn't want to go out with me.
You know, Ethan's a cool guy and all, he's just kind of—
Duhhhh...
Yeah, but knowing that someone's wrong for you doesn't change the way you feel.

How much do I owe you?
It's on the house—I'm out of business. Sonny Mazerowski shut me down.
Life's unfair.
You said it, sister. You said it.
Hey. How're you doing?
Oh, not bad. My parents kept pulling the "any guy would be lucky to go out with you" thing.
You wanna go to the dance anyway?

Nah. I don't have a date.
Neither do I. I thought of someone I could ask, but it turns out Brad Pitt's married.
And, as predicted, poor old Gordo got zero invites. The big goose egg. Good morning, good afternoon, and good night.
So...dance with *me*.
Play it, Lanny.
C'mon. Let's go.

I may not have a date, but I am not gonna be the wallflower.
For the record, I think you're much better at being Lizzie than at being Ethan's type.
Yeah, well, it was fun for a while, but I think I would have gotten sick of not being me.
See, if I were still "Ethan's type," I would have no idea how to do this...
WOOSH!

AHA!
Well, I like you better as you. Although that mystery woman thing was kind of—
Oh, you think so?
Isn't that what I just said?
Did you? Did you really?
The End

Take Lizzie home!
THE
WALT DISNEY PICTURES PRESENTS
LIZZIE McGUIRE
MOVIE
CINE-MANGA™
AVAILABLE IN JULY!
Y
YOUTH AGE 7+
© 2004 DISNEY ENTERPRISES INC. ALL RIGHTS RESERVED.
www.TOKYOPOP.com
TOKYOPOP®

TOKYOPOP®
that's so raven™
The future is now!
The hit show from Disney is now a hot new Cine-Manga™!
A ALL AGES
©Disney Enterprises, Inc. ©2004 TOKYOPOP Inc. All Rights Reserved.
www.TOKYOPOP.com

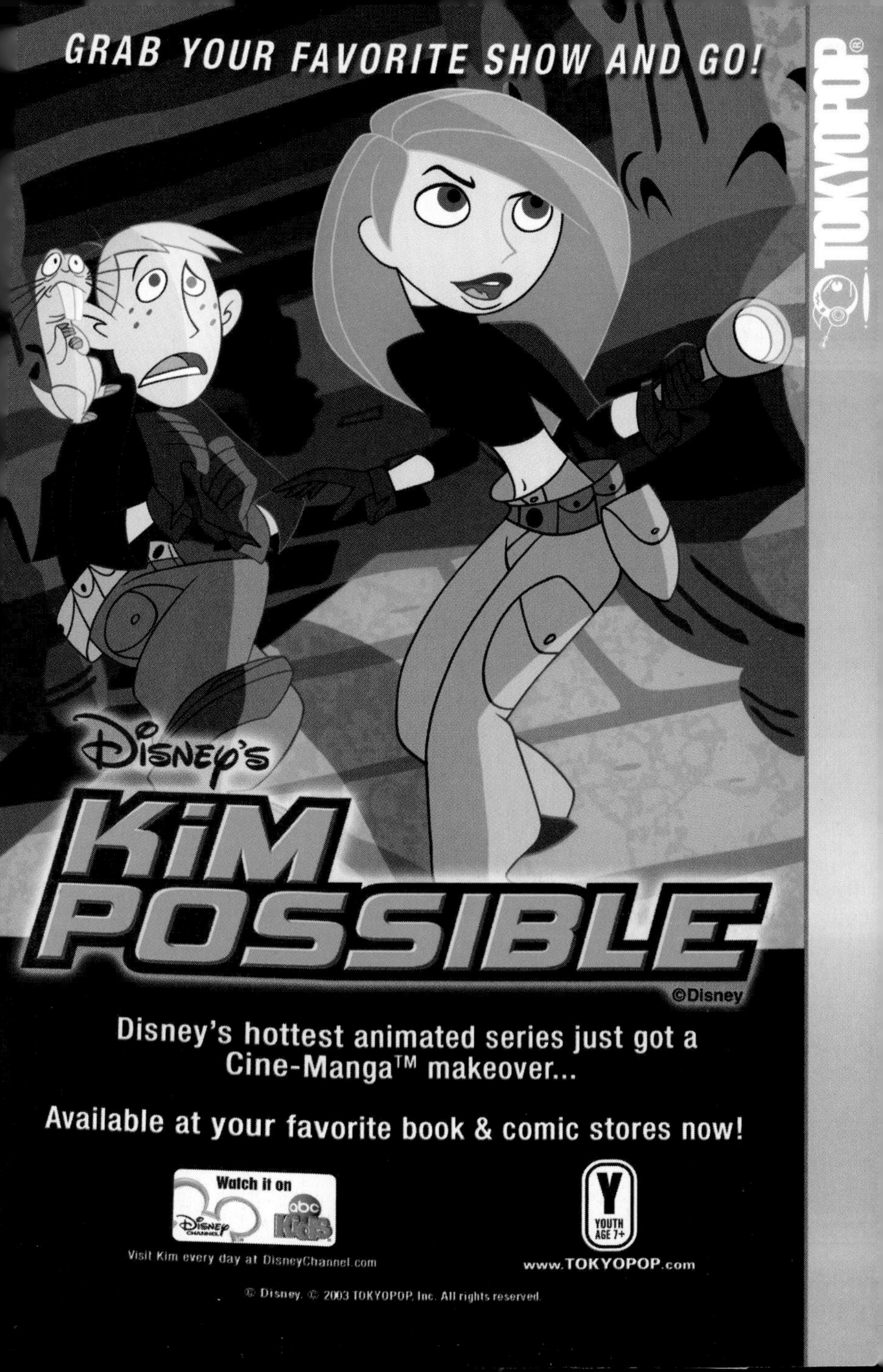
GRAB YOUR FAVORITE SHOW AND GO!
TOKYOPOP
DISNEY'S
KIM POSSIBLE
©Disney
Disney's hottest animated series just got a Cine-Manga™ makeover...
Available at your favorite book & comic stores now!
Watch it on
DISNEY CHANNEL
abc Kids
Visit Kim every day at DisneyChannel.com
Y
YOUTH AGE 7+
www.TOKYOPOP.com
© Disney. © 2003 TOKYOPOP, Inc. All rights reserved.

3 Enchanting Films Of Magic And Adventure

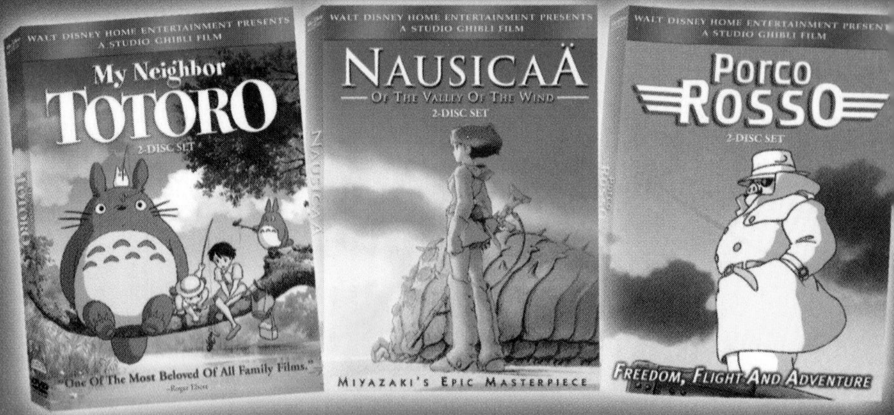

First Time On 2-Disc DVD

Available August 21

OM
IYAZAKI
Of The
rd®-Winning*
Away

7/11

ok

cks

Miya